The Journal of Abigail Langley

Of Nansemond County, Virginia

So-called in the family, but properly:

"John Granbery, Junior, His Book, 1708"

Prepared for publication by

Alice Granbery Walter

CLEARFIELD

Printed for Clearfield Company by
Genealogical Publishing Company
Baltimore, Maryland
2011

ISBN 978-0-8063-5555-9

Made in the United States of America

THESE EXCERPTS FROM THE JOURNAL OF ABIGAIL LANGLEY

so-called in the family, but properly:

"JOHN GRANBERY, JUNIOR HIS BOOK, 1708"

Originally owned by:
"JOHN CHILLCOTT, his book 1694" and in his possession until 8 Feby 1696
to
JOHN GRANBERY (13) 1708
to
his wife
ABIGAIL GRANBERY in 1733
to
her daughter
MARY GRANBERY COWPER (16) 1763
to
her nephew
JOHN GRANBERY (25) 1806
to his son
HENRY AUGUSTUS THADEUS GRANBERY (55) 1815
to his grandson
JULIAN HASTINGS GRANBERY (211) 1904
to a distant cousin
WILLIAM LANGLEY GRANBERY (372) 1961
presented to the
VIRGINIA HISTORICAL SOCIETY 1963
Richmond, Virginia

(The numbers in brackets represent the numbers assigned to these persons in the book, "John Granbery, Virginia" by Julian Hastings Granbery 1964)

TO USE THIS TRANSCRIPT
REFER TO ORIGINAL BOOK
BEGINNING ON PAGE 26

The Journal of Abigail Langley
OF NANSEMOND COUNTY, VIRGINIA

•

So-called in the family, but properly:
"JOHN GRANBERY, JUNIOR, HIS BOOK, 1708"

•

The book referred to as the Journal of Abigail Langley is a small (3¼ x 7¼) volume of fifty-seven numbered pages (originally, twenty-two, eight leaves had been cut out before 1807) bound in stiff, white tooled skin with a flap and a bronze clasp. John Chillcott, the first owner, used the book for some accounts in Nansemond County in 1694 and after, but it passed from him to John Granbery, Junior, at sometime between 1695 and 1723.

The book descended from John Granbery Junior to his widow in 1733, from Abigail Hargroves (his widow, remarried) to their daughter, Mary Granbery Cowper (16). She gave it, in 1806, to her nephew, John Granbery (25) of Virginia, at whose death in 1815 to his son, Henry Augustus Thaddeus Granbery (55), who left it to his grand-son, Julian Hastings Granbery (211), the author of John Granbery, Va.

The preceding commentary was written by Julian Hastings Granbery in 1946, and in that same year he presented it to William Langley Granbery (372) of Brentwood, Tennessee, the third of that name and the seventh in line of descent from John Granbery, Jr. and Abigail Langley. The latter presented it to the Virginia Historical Society, Richmond, Virginia in 1963 where it may be safely retained for the perusal of future generations.

This little book was the inspiration to the author for the genealogy of John Granbery, Va. and furnished the proof needed, with other original records, to document fifteen generations of this family.

Dr. E. G. Swem commented in a letter written to me 29 March 1963: "I know of no other journal, that is a diary, of any Virginia woman of the Colonial period;" and in a letter 16 April 1963: "I have looked over your father's manuscript of The Journal, and you could have no better copy for a printer. I would leave the quotation marks as he has placed them indicating what is in The Journal, and his running comment.

The original journal without omissions and annotated with a running commentary of its contents. Genealogical facts connected with the Langley, Mason and Thelaball families of Virginia who were the progenitors of Abigail Langley will be included.

ALICE GRANBERY WALTER
Publisher

THE JOURNAL OF ABIGAIL LANGLEY
(of Nansemond County)

The book referred to as the Journal of Abigail Langley is a small (3¼" x 7½") volume of 57 numbered pages (originally 72, 8 leaves had been cut out before 1807) bound in stiff, white, tooled skin with a flap and a bronze clasp. John Chilcott, the first owner, was a convicted rebel, consigned to the Barbadoes Oct. 24, 1685 by frigate John, Capt. Will States Commander. He was from Tiverton in Devonshire and used the book for some accounts in Nansemond County in 1694 and after but it passed from him to John Granbery, Junior, at some time between 1695 and 1723.

The book descended from

John Granbery Jr. to his widow Abigail in 1733, from Abigail Hargroves (his widow, remarried) to his daughter Mary Granbery Cowper who gave it, in 1806, to her nephew John Granbery of Virginia, at whose death in 1815 it passed to his son Henry Augustus Thaddeus Granbery, who left it to Julian Hastings Granbery (who writes this) grandson of H.A.T. Granbery. It is now in the possession of William Langley Granbery of Brentwood, Tenn. the third of that name and the seventh in line of descent from John Granbery Jr. and Abigail Langley.

The spelling and the arrangement of items on the following pages follow, as nearly as possible, that in the original. Where dashes are used in a few names the ink has faded out to such an extent that it cannot be deciphered, even by fuming.

J. H. Granbery

November 26, 1946

THE JOURNAL OF ABIGAIL LANGLEY
(of Nansemond County)

The book referred to as the Journal of Abigail Langley is a small (3½" × 7½") volume of 57 numbered pages (originally 72, 8 leaves had been cut out before 1807) bound in stiff, white, tooled skin with a flap and a bronze clasp. John Chilcott, the first owner, was a convicted rebel, consigned to the Barbadoes Oct. 24, 1685 by frigate John, Capt. Kill States Commander. He was from Tiverton in Devonshire and used the book for some accounts in Nansemond County in 1694 and after but it passed from him to John Granbery, Junior, at some time between 1685 and 1723.

The book descended from

John Granbery Jr. to his widow Abigail in 1733, from
Abigail Hargraves (his widow, remarried) to his daughter
Mary Granbery Cowper who gave it, in 1806, to her nephew
John Granbery of Virginia, at whose death in 1815 it passed to his son
Henry Augustus Thaddeus Granbery, who left it to
Julian Hastings Granbery (who writes this) grandson of H.A.T. Granbery

It is now in the possession of William Langley Granbery of Brentwood, Tenn. the third of that name and the seventh in line of descent from John Granbery Jr. and Abigail Langley.

The spelling and the arrangement of items on the following pages follow, as nearly as possible, that in the original. Where dashes are used in a few names the ink has faded out to such an extent that it cannot be deciphered, even by fuming.

J. H. Granbery

November 26, 1946

19 March 1963

Dear Mr. Granbery:

It gives me much pleasure again to address someone with that surname, for I was exceedingly fond of your late kinsman, Mr. Julian Hastings Granbery. The opportunity to address you, moreover, on the following subject gives me ever greater pleasure, for I have long been familiar, through the late Mr. Granbery and his daughter, Mrs. Walter, with the Abigail Langley Journal. It is deeply gratifying to us to receive this valued manuscript for the Society's library.

On behalf of our Executive Committee I extend to you our collective thanks for your kindness and interest in presenting the volume to our library. It will be carefully catalogued and preserved along with the other manuscript materials which constitute our most precious holdings. The volume reached our hands via our good friend, Mrs. Walter, this morning.

With warmest good wishes, I am

Sincerely yours,

John Melville Jennings
Director

William Langley Granbery III, Esq.
725 Darden Place
Nashville 5, Tennessee

✓ Copy to Mrs. Maurice Walter   *A million thanks & yrs. — sincerely, JMJ*

4

JOURNAL OF ABIGAIL LANGLEY

On outside of front cover: "1694" (the ink is faded and looks more like 1614).

On inside of front cover: (handwriting of Abigail Hargroves, as she then was)

" in april 1746 boty inkins came to me "

"September 28 sister was   1746"
the line has been blotted out by streak of ink across it (evidently the same with which it was written) and the word before 1746 is undecipherable though it looks as if it might have been the word "born." The space is too short for the word "buried."

"1743 december the 5 day william granbery went Away the last time to go too norfort "

"november 22 cutler runaway with billey to norfort an Stoal his Cloes like a rogue as he was - 1748 "

At top of page 1: "John Chillcott His Booke 1694"
Along the binding edge, at right angles to Chillcott's writing: (handwriting of Abigail Hargroves)
" Mr. Jones minnester of the loer parrish died July the 29 day in the year 1742 on Saterday an died suddenly "

On page 2: illegible accounts in Chillcott's writing, then
"John Chillcott "in his writing, followed by "What is the name of me John Granbery"
"one hog^d of tob^a " in the same writing
"— illice " in an unknown hand and
"— por boddis " in another unknown hand
" mr. Jones died " at the bottom of the page.

At top of page 3: "foabruary ye 8th 1695 6
bort of John noyatt for Mr Thruston one
hd of tobackoo grosd 580 two 8b. VE. J.C.

January ye 28 1695 6 Robort Horning Retnd
one hd of tobb. for mr Thruston:of Abraham
Edwards for the acct of Robort Bayley waying grass
500 livre 71: "

The other accounts are crossed off. The entire
page is in Chillcott's writing.

At top of page 4: "John Granbery Detr
to Christopher wigall 4~6
Christopher wigall Detr
to one pen nife 8 8d
to one half a yard of Calaco 2/6
to one half a yd of Canlo Sones 4 ☞
Wigall's account is crossed off.
All in John Granbery's handwriting.

At top of page 5: "Roda draper deter in 1708
to fouor yards of whitt lenen att   0 8 0
one yd of stript lenen   0 5 6
one yard and half of whitt lenen more   0 4 5
to blue lenen   0 1 8
one pare of gloufes   0 1 8
                                        _____
                                        2, 17 "

In unknown handwriting; the account has
been crossed off.
Below it is written :- "John Gran—
Bery Junor his
Book God him
Grace thereIn to
Look Amen "

At top of page 6: unknown handwriting
"Goorg ash. 1 Gall of Sider
Charls Robarts 2½ Gall sider
Thomas Roling 1 Gall of Sider
hugh Montgomery ?) huemand gumery 2 Gall of sider "
Above it, in the handwriting of John Granbery
"oho The heavens Dew" as if written later.

At top of page 7:   "John Gran Bery his
                        Book God Give his Grace
                        Therein to Look & he
                        Seals this book from
                        me Deserves to be
                        hanged on A tree"

The balance of the page has accounts which
have been crossed out.

At top, across pages 8 and 9:" Edward Clark
        to three bushels and a peck of Indian Corn at 6$\underline{9}$
        to one Tobacco hogshd — — — — at 2 6 "

At top of page 10: "John Granbery and
        to one days work at 30
        to one half of dito at 12 "

" Dearals th
Dear cossne eti com to let Know " in an unformed
handwriting like that of a child.

```
"  90..   11 . 0
   57..    0 .9
   22...    1 . 4
   19 ..   14 . 4
    6 .     8 . 0
   10 .     0 . 0
    3 .     0 . 10
   ─────────────
  208 : 16 — 3
  298    12 . 10
   ─────────────
   90     3 . 5
   40 .    0    0
   ─────────────
   50 . 3    5  "
```

= John Hargroves

In John Hargrove's writing

Upside down between the two foregoing but in
John Hargroves writing :

```
"  15 . 0 . 0
   17 . 0 . 0
    1 . 5 . 0
   ─────────────
   33 .. 5 .. 0
```

outstanding Dets Recovered "

One leaf (2 pages) torn out between 10 and 11

On page 11: in John Hargroves writing

" 0 ·· 8 ·· 6
0 · 4 · 0
4 · 1 · 0
5 · 0 · 6
5 · 2 · 0
5 · 0 · 0
4 · 12 · 6
30 · 10 · 0
0 · 3 · 6
———————
55 · 10 · 0
1 · 10 · 9
———————
£ 57 · 0 · 9

"Things Bought at the sail"

16 ·· 14 · 4
6 · 8 —
90 · 11. ———
22 · 1 · 4
3 · 0 · 10
10 · 0 · 0

298 ·· 12 ·· 10
208 · 16 · 3
———————
99   16 ·· 7   "

At top of page 12: "Hous fraim bought of
Mʳ Sturnour" in John
Hargroves writing ··

At top of page 13: " 298 · 12 · 10
208 · 16 · 3
———————
90 · 16 ·· 7
35 ·· 6 · 7
———————
55 ·· 10 · 0 "

" 90 · 16 · 7 "

in John Hargroves' writing.

Page 14 is blank.

At top of page 15: "Deare cosen the " in the
Same unformed writing as on page 10.
Below it, in John Hargroves writing:

"Steven
Howard   0..5..0
            0..12.0
            0..5.6
 40.0.0   0.8.6
            1.16.9
           ―――――――
            3.7.9

 20.5.0
  6.11.4
―――――――――
13..13.8 "

"Dear Sir please to send"
in another (unknown)
hand writing.

=

"To To J J".

At top of page 16: "mary Coufew"   (Mary Cowper?)
"to one Tobo hogh at―30
to one half hoeh ― 12
    James B ― "
all in unknown handwriting. Directly
below it:

" May the 23th day 1733
Sambo my negro boy was Judged by
the Court to be eight years of age
        John Granbery "

On page 17 :

" Memo. made by John Granbery in Norfolk 23d June 1812

Josiah Granbery, second son of Josiah Granbery & Christian his wife was born 15 Aug. 1764 married Elizabeth Cowper, who was born in Nansemond 8 Dec. 1766 - & married the 17 Jany 1784

their children

Christian -- 16 may 1785 at Suffolk
Louis --- 19 Jany 1788 " carolina
William Francis 12 Mar 1790 " nancemond
Josiah Allen 1 Sept. 1792 died 21 Oct. 1799
[Gilby] Grissey ---- 3 Nov. 1797,
Richd Allen ·· 3 Oct 1802, Norfolk
Mary or Polly 20 Apr. 1795.
John Gregory 27 Aug. 1807 norfo County
Elizabeth 27 Nov. 1804 do.

Josiah Granbery the father of the above, died decr. 12. 1811 & Elizabeth his wife died 9 March 1812 both buried at their plantation near Hall's mill. "

At top of page 18 : in the same hand writing as page 17

James Granbery was the third son of Josiah & Christian Granbery - was born

and married Mary Harvey, daughter of Col. Thos. Harvey of Perquimans, on the 31 May 1796 - they had children

Mary   born 23 Nov. 1797 died
Charles   13 Oct. 1800 "
Margaret 18 Apr. 1805

James died in Edenton Oct. 1804.

Page 19 is blank.

10

At the top of page 20:

"Augusta Granbery's —
written by her great
-grandmother- by her
father's side —"

2 leaves (4 pages) torn out between 20 and 21

Page 21 is blank.

At the top of page 22:

" marcy lord Grant us marcy lor
deare this coms to let yo kn "

in the unformed writing of pp. 10 and 15

Below it in the handwriting of page 17 (John Granbery 1759-1815)

"Josiah Granbery second son of Josiah Granbery was born
15 Augt. 1764 married Elizabeth Cowper who was born in
Nansemond 8 Decr 1766, were married 17 Jany 1784. —
            Their Children

Christian G.	born	16 May 1785
Louis . . .	"	19 Jany 1788
William Francis	"	12 Mar. 1790
Josiah Allen	"	1 Sept. 1792 died Oct 1799
Gilby . . .	"	3 Nov. 1797
Richard Allen	"	3 Oct. 1802
Mary or Polly	"	20 Apr. 1795
John Gregory	"	27 Aug. 1807
Betsey . . .	"	27 Nov. 1804 died 1818

Josiah the father of the above died Dec. 12, 1811 at his
plantation on Western Branch Norfk Co. and his widow
died at same place 9 March 1812

Suffolk burned by the British troops 13 May 1779 "

Written across this last item is : "Ann Grambry" in
a hand which looks like that of one of the negroes
that was being taught to write. It is of a much later
date to judge from the ink.

11

At the top of page 23:

"written in 1806 by John Granbery

+ Josiah Granbery left Nansemond 21 Oct. 1747 to go & keep store in Chowan now Gates County for Riddick supposed Col. Leml Riddick — after this he kept store at the Folly for his own acct, then at the place now called Sunsbury, which he purchased, about 7 miles on the south side of the Virginia line where John & Polly were born — about the year 1776 the family moved to Suffolk; he — entered into trade with James Gibson, in Suffolk were born Josiah & James. — See the Family Bible.

John married Susanna B. Stowe of Bermuda 23 Sept. 1789 — lived in Norfolk from 1790 —

Their Children

Betsey born 13 April 1791 married Jonas Hastings Aug. 1810.
George " 9 Sept. 1794
Julia " 17 Jany. 1797
Polly " 11 Mar. 1793 died Oct. 1804
John Gregory 10 Oct. 1798 died 4 Aug. 1799
Caroline 3 Sept. 1800
Augusta 2 May 1802
Henrietta 2 Sept. 1804 died 9 May 1807
Mary — 6 April 1806
Henry Augustus 24 March 1808
John Stowe H. 27 Sept. 1811 died 20 Oct. 1814 "

The underlined portions are in ink that is less faded than the rest and were evidently written by the same hand at a later date

12

Pages 24 and 25 are blank.

At the top of page 26: in the handwriting of "John Granbery Dotr" (at the top of page 4, whi [see]).

"John Granbory was married to abigail Langley the 26 Day of febuary 172$\frac{2}{3}$

———————

Thomas Granbery son of John Granbery and abigail his wife was born the twenty fourth day of June 1724

———————

* Mary Granbery daughter of John Gran and abigail his wife was born the eight day of april 1726

———————

+ Josiah Granbery son of John Granbory and abigail his wife was born the 14th day of October 1728 "

———————

In the handwriting of John Granbory (1759-1815) under april 1726 : "died Jany 7 1814 nearly 88 years old, widow of John Cowper the father of Wills John & Robert by a first wife " under October 1728 : "died at Suffolk Decr 1772"

"+ The father of John Granbery, the writer of above in the City of Norfolk July 1813 "

born
(8 years before she married John Jr.) "page perrin April 1715" in what looks like the handwriting of Abigail Langley.

At the top of page 27: John Granbery Detr continues
"John Granbery son of John Granbery and abigail his wife was born the third day of october 1730

———————

William Granbery Son of John Granbery and abigail his wife was born the twenty third day of march 173$\frac{1}{2}$"

———————

" Margreat Granbery daughter of John Granbory and abigail his wife was born the twenty Saesn day of September 1733
In the year 1733 my dear an loving husband departed this lief on the 25 day of desember
                              Abigail Granbery "
"Note, has been married about 10 years "
written by John Granbery (1759-1815)

13

On page 28 : handwriting of Abigail Hargroves

" hillary hargroves son of Robert hargroves and
Abigail his wief was born the 6 day of march 173$\frac{6}{7}$

On page 29 : continuation

"Abigail Langley hargroves daughter of Robert
hargroves and Abigail his wief was born august
the twenty day 1738 <u>an died 19 of october 1747</u>

Marg hargroves was born (scratched out)

Margreat hargroves was born September the
fifth day 1740

and died the 30 day of october 1740

hillary hargrove died 2 day of november 1743 "

On page 30 : handwriting of Abigail Hargroves

" november the 10 day Willies Hargroves was
born 1741
bety Jenkins Born July 21 1743
an came to me april 1748

pagge granbery born october the 6 day 1752
John granbery born november the 1 day 1755
Josiah granbery born march the 14 1754
(written across the last three by John Granbery
1759-1815 " These were the children of John Granbery")
my dear mother departed this lief november
19 day 1738
                Abigail Hargroves "

On page 31 : " my dear father departed this lief
the 5 day of october 1747
my father born desember 1654 an died
october the 5 day 1747
my mother born august 1660 an died
november the 19 day 1738
                Abigail Hargroves "

Page 32 is blank.

14

On page 33:

"John Granbery the Son of John Granbery was
Borne in the year of Our Lord 1755
November the 1 day
Peggy Granbery Was Born in the Year of 1752
October the 6 Day

Peggy Granbery Was born Oct. 6th Day in
the year of our Lord & Christ 1752"
Handwriting unidentified.

At the top of page 34:
directly across from the
item on the facing page

"The father of William,
Wills, John, Robert &
Gilby or Guzzel Cowper."

written by John Granbery
1759-1815

At the bottom of page 34;
written upside down:

"John Brower
1794 To Mary Cowper Dr.
To damage in Cornfield
by horses ——— £ 3 . --
Josiah Pinner
1793 To Mary Cowper Dr.
To 1 Cow & Calf £ 3 " — " -
1796 To 1 heffer   2 " 2 "
                   ————
                   £ 5 " 2 "
Handwriting of Mary Granbery Cowper
Page 36 is blank

At the top of page 35:
facing page 34

" John Cowper
departed this life
May 22nd 1768 "
——— * ———
" Abigall Hargroves
Wife of Robert Har-
groves departed this
life Feby 29th 1763 "

both in the same, unknown,
handwriting

15

On page 37; continued on page 39:

" ✳ This John Cowper was the father of William,
Wills, John, Robert & Gilby Cowper – His second
wife was Mary Granbery born 8 April 1726 – Now
alive, – (my old Aunt Cowper) near Suffolk. –
William Cowper was married to my mother in 1777
or thereabouts, she then being the widow Doeber.
Abigail Hargroves was the wife of my Grandfather
John Granbery. – They lived
(on page 39) near Hargroves, now Huttons (could be
read as Hattons) Mills, the House was off the
road, on the Mill run – this was the plantation
or estate. – It appears that he John Granbery
was a planter & trader – that the farm produced
Tobacco in those days – Hogsheads of 400 to 500
pounds –

= This book my old aunt Cowper gave to me in
1806. It appears to be written by my Grandmother
Abigail Granbery whose maiden name was Langley,
see page 26.
In December 1733 my Grandfather died, – his
widow married Robert Hargroves - - - They
had children, see page 28. –
John Granbery, born
7 Oct. 1759 "

Upside down at bottom of page 39:
"To outstanding Debts Recovered - - - -
To one account of "
handwriting of John Granbery Jr.

On page 38; along margin:
" Augusta Ellen Granbery "
June 11th, 1820 - Sunday -
in her writing, the rest of page is blank.

16

At top of page 40:
" marten Grambry
Ann Grambry
jaggy grambru her "

which appear to have
been written by negro
children owned by
Abigail Hargroves.

On page 41:
Scrawls, evidently the work of the above.

On page 42:
" Lucs my negro boy born desember the 29 1745 A H

Charls negro boey was born the 6 day of
october 1747   A H

Rachel my negro gal was born november the
2 day 1749

Jams was born the 5 of Juen 1752

Jack an Sam was born march the 15 the
too tweens 1755

Sele an trece was born September the 5
the too tweens 1757

Abigail Hargroves "

On page 43; in the same handwriting
" Juen the 26 day my neogro boy martan
was born 1760 "

"desember the 5 day 1761
mary Granbery died

desember 22 day 1761
littel Abisba caeme hear to live "

probably the same writer using a finer
quill, the characters are much lighter
and the strokes more delicate.

On page 44; at bottom, upside down :

" Memorāndum
to Enquired for Spurne's bill of sale
from Will Cox on the Rekrds
from yᵉ year 1660
backward to 1640 "
writer not identified.

" Sold the 25 march 1728
to one Stick at   1-3
to one pair of sho   2-6 "
a different writer but likewise unidentified.

On page 45; at bottom, upside down

"July 25th 1723
Deᵗʳ to Phill Runel
to peʳ of phis at ___ 1-0
to one Ɔblis at ___ 2-3
to one yd of Rem at ___ 10

Detʳ to James Mac-
600 pound of tocboo
Paid 551 ─ 49 Duu
_____

Due to John Granbery Juner 5
_____

Due to moses Granbery
to one _____ 5 "

The accounts are all crossed off, they
are in a hand somewhat like that of John
Granbery Jr. but in blacker ink and not so
well formed.

On page 46:

Many names and many gallons of "Sider" and Cider
all crossed off and written over so that they
are hard to identify. Not all in the same writing.

On page 47:

Crossed out accounts, writer unidentified

On page 48:

Colored (red) pencil curlicues of the names Robert Sarah Roger Roberts

On page 49:

"Box money" and crossed out names and amounts (in pencil). No familiar names, and not very legible. Unknown writing

On page 50:

(Peele?)
"John peoel Dettor to Sarah Granbery
to 2 pound of Butter at —12
nine pound of tobacco
to 2 Gall of Sider at —— 16
to 2 Gall of Sider more at— 16
to 2½ Gallans of Sider more at— 20
to 2 Gallans of Sider more at — 16
to 1 Galla of Sider more at —— 08
to 1 pound of Butter at —— 06
to 1 peack of meal ————— 10 "

all crossed off, the same handwriting as page 45

On page 51:

"Thomas Brickel
To one pot and hooks
To one pesol
To one bar iron "

better writing, more like that of John Granbery Jr. but still uncertain.

On page 47:

Crossed out accounts, writer unidentified

On page 48:

Colored (red) pencil curlicues of the
names Robert Sarah Roger Roberts

On page 49:

" Box money" and crossed out names
and amounts (in pencil). No familiar names,
and not very legible. Unknown writing

On page 50:

(Peele?)   " John pooel Dettor to Sarah Granbery
      to 2 pound of Butter at - 12
        nine pound of tobacco
    to 2 Gall of Sider at —— 16
    to 2 Gall of Sider more at 16
    to 2½ Gallans of Sider more at 20
    to 2 Gallans of Sider more at — 16
    to 1 Galla of Sider more at —— 08
    to 1 pound of Butter at ——— 06
    to 1 peack of meal ———————— 10. "

all crossed off, the same handwriting as page 45

On page 51:

" Thomas Brickel
    To one pot and hooks
    To one pesol
    To one bar iron "
    better writing, more like that of John
    Granbery Jr. but still uncertain.

Page 20 appears to be a duplicate of page 19.

On page 52:

"John Peoel Detts

to one Gallan & half of Sider —— at 12

to one three Pound of Chees at —— 21

to one peck of wheat at $12\frac{1}{2}$

to one half pound of butter ——— at 03

to one Gall of Sider ——————— at 08

to one Gall of Sider at 08

to one pottel of Sider at 04

to one pottel of Sider 04
————

    John peoel Ditto $72\frac{1}{2}$

to one Gallan & half of Sider   12

one pottel of Sider   4

to one hoe   12

        All crossed off.

"The account of Corne Three bushels and half of Corn"

        "faberary 1739"

At top of page 53;

    "an acount of Corne payd to James Mack
    three bushels Carred hooue
    two bushels paid to my moter
    two bushels for yalls son
    five bushels to thomas mane
                Auggust 27 1716"

The rest of page 53 is upside down and a continuation, in the same (similar) handwriting, of page 54. (Chillcott?)

On page 54; upside down; badly faded and
almost illegible:

"   ——   wher—
    ——   for
the year 1694
    E——   Ben—
• William Sumne one pa—
John Evans one paire
Henry Sky-me one paire
• John Knoles one paire
Abraham Bryant one pair
• Hugh Logan one paire
• Wm Edwards one paire
Robert Steward one paire
• Tho: Corbell one paire
Edward Hughs one paire
John wayatt one paire
• a.bm. Woodly one paire
John Brassinere one paire
• John Keeson one paire
Tho: Jordan one paire
• Gressham Cofield one paire
Robert Jordan one paire "

continuing on page 53:
• " Andrew —— ne one paire
Richard Sanders for his sister
Mallory Th——
Henry Plumon one paire
• Wm Wright one paire
John Forteis one paire
• Richard Korney one paire
John Walth one paire
• Richard Walridge one paire
Wm. Granbery Jun.r one pr "

All in Chillcotts handwriting; most of the names
have been crossed out, those marked • have not been.

" Mr Thomas Boue
Deter 8 Gall of Sider "

On page 55; written along and down the
outer margin by Abigail Hargroves:

"Sears Langley went away fabury 9 day 1739"

On page 56: "9160"

"John Granbery his Book and in it let
him Look
John Granbery

1788
1726
62

20

Gorilla

hunny and corry but When henny hisitop
corry is corn and pick is corn
MG

On page 57; which is the inside of the back cover:

"Josiah went from hear the 21 day of october to
goo to Cariliner to keep Stoer for Redock 1747

Sary hancok begin to wef the 29 day of
october her first web of lase 1747 "

the handwriting is that of Abigail Hargroves.

To be added to

THE JOURNAL OF ABIGAIL LANGLEY

There appear to have been two different men named John Chilcot or Chillcott:

JOHN CHILCOT of Tiverton in Devon Shire, a convicted rebel, "attainted of high Treason... Shipt at Bristoll on the John frigget cap. Will: Stokes (or Stoakes)" dated Dorchester Oct. 24, 1685. Certified as delivered to the Barbadoes and sold to Ann Gallop Feby. 1, 1686.

(Original Lists, Hotten, pp. 334, 337, 341).

JOHN CHILCOTT of Nansemond County, Va., was a party to "The Humble petition of J^{no}: Chilcott and James Hay Churchwardens of the Lower parish of Nantmond County on the behalfe of ye parish afforesaid" to the "Right Hon^{n}abl^e S^r: William Berkley" for a "survey and ffarther confirmation of a gleabe" and therefore in or before 1677 when Berkeley relinquished the government and returned to England.

(Original petition, discovered in "Colonial Papers" in Va. State Archives in December 1947).

JOHN CHILCOT of Nansemond Co., by order of the General Court dated Apr. 16, 1692, was granted 220 acres of land formerly granted to William Coepheld (Cofield) and John Granbery Apr. 24, 1682 "and by them deserted" on Apr. 29, 1693.

(Patent Book 8, p. 279, Va. State Land Office).

"JOHN CHILLCOTT his Book 1694" on page 1 of the book, and his account on page 3 indicate that the book was in his possession until Feby. 8, 1696.

The land grant of 220 acres, or at least 75 acres upon which Ann Granbery paid "Rent Roll for the year 1704," remained in the tenure and occupation of the Granbery family until the death of John Granbery, husband of Abigail Langley, in December, 1733 (probably until 1772 when John, their son, who lived on or near it, died).

J. W. Granbery, Feby. 10, 1948.

To be added to

THE JOURNAL OF ABIGAIL LANGLEY

There appear to have been two different men named John Chilcot or Chillcott:

JOHN CHILCOT of Tiverton in Devon Shire, a convicted rebel, "attainted of high Treason ··· Shipt at Bristoll on the John frigget cap. Will: Stokes (or Stoakes)" dated Dorchester Oct. 24, 1685. Certified as delivered to the Barbadoes and sold to Ann Gallop Feby. 1, 1686.

(Original Lists, Hotten, pp. 334, 337, 341).

JOHN CHILLCOTT of Nansemond County, Va., was a party to "The Humble petition of Jno: Chillcott and James Hay Church-wardens of the Lower parish of Nantmond County on the behalfe of ye parish afforesaid" to the "Right Honrable Sr: William Berkley" for a "survey and fðarther confirmation of a gleabe" and therefore in or before 1677 when Berkeley relinquished the government and returned to England.

(Original petition, discovered in "Colonial Papers" in Va. State Archives in December 1947).

JOHN CHILCOT of Nansemond Co., by order of the General Court dated Apr. 16, 1692, was granted 220 acres of land formerly granted to William Coepheld (Cofield) and John Granbery Apr. 24, 1682 "and by them deserted" on Apr. 29, 1693.

(Patent Book 8, p. 279, Va. State Land Office).

"JOHN CHILLCOTT his Book 1694" on page 1 of the book, and his account on page 3 indicate that the book was in his possession until Feby. 8, 1696.

The land grant of 220 acres, or at least 75 acres of it upon which Ann Granbery paid "Rent Roll for the year 1704," remained in the tenure and occupation of the Granbery family until the death of John Granbery, husband of Abigail Langley, in December, 1733 (probably until 1772 when John, their son, who lived on or near it, died).

J. W. Granbery, Feby. 10, 1948.

25

firck of Indian Corn at 6 .. 6 .. "
— — — — — at 2 6 .

8 .... wholly and 6 ..
to three tobacco
to one togyther
φ one to Co Coy
φ of
adam Coen

149 —

Hous frame bought of
Mr Sturmont

50

248·12·10
200·16·3
90·16·7
35·6·7
55·10·0

90·16·7

15

James Franklyn was
the third son of ...
& Christian Edinburgh — was
born

and maria Mary
Henry daughter of Ald...
the ... of ... — ...
#53 may 1796. — they
had Children

Mary ...... born 23 Nov 1757 and
Charles .. 13 oct 1800 "
Margaret : 18 apr 1565

* James died in Calcutta oct 1804

Augusta Granberry —
written by her great
— grand mother
[illegible]

John Granbory Son of
John granbory and
abigail by wife was
born the third Day of
october 1730

William Granbory son
of John granbory and
Abigail his wife was
born the twenty third
Day of march 1731

Margreat Granbery
Daughter of John
Granbery and abigail
his wife was born the
twenty six ... of
december 1732

Sn the year 1733

John Granbery was
married to Ethered
Langton the 28 Day
of february 1722/3

Thomas Granbery Son
John Granbery and
abigail his wife was
born the twenty fourth
Day of June 1724

Mary Granbery
Daughter of John Granbery
and abigail his wife
was born this eighth day
of april 1726

Josiah Granbery
Son of John granbery
and abigaie his wife
was born the 14 Day
of october 1728

Abigail Longley

Hargraves Daughter
of Robert Hargraves
and Abigail his
wife was born
august fiten day
1738 and died 19
october 1747

Margaret Hargraves
was born

Margaret Hargraves
was born to inlow
the eight day 1740

and died the 30 day
of october 1740

Hillary hargraves
son of Robert
hargraves and
Abigail his wife
was born the 6 day
of march 1735/6
1743

my Dear father Depar
rtit Lies Hargroues
ted this Lief the 5 Day
of october 1747

was Born 1745

Betty Jarkins Born
July 21 1743

an Cage ... may april 1746
Page ... very ...
october ... 6 Day 1752

John grat ... very born
november ... the 1 Day
Josiah ... July 1755
Born march the 14 1745 ... august 16..

my Dear mother departe
this Lief november 19
Day 1738
Abigail Hargroues

my father born
Setember 1654
and die octobe ... in Lett..
my mother born
the august 16.
Die november
the 19 Day 1738
Abigail Hargroues

33

John Granberry
The son of John
Granberry was
Born in the year
of Thursday 1735 —
November the 13 Day

Peggy Granberry
was Born in the
Year of 1758.
October the 6 Day

32

Peggy Granberry
... was ...
... 6 ...

John Cowper
departed this life
May 22nd, 1768 ―

Abigail Hargroves

1763

Josiah Kinnis
1793
1796

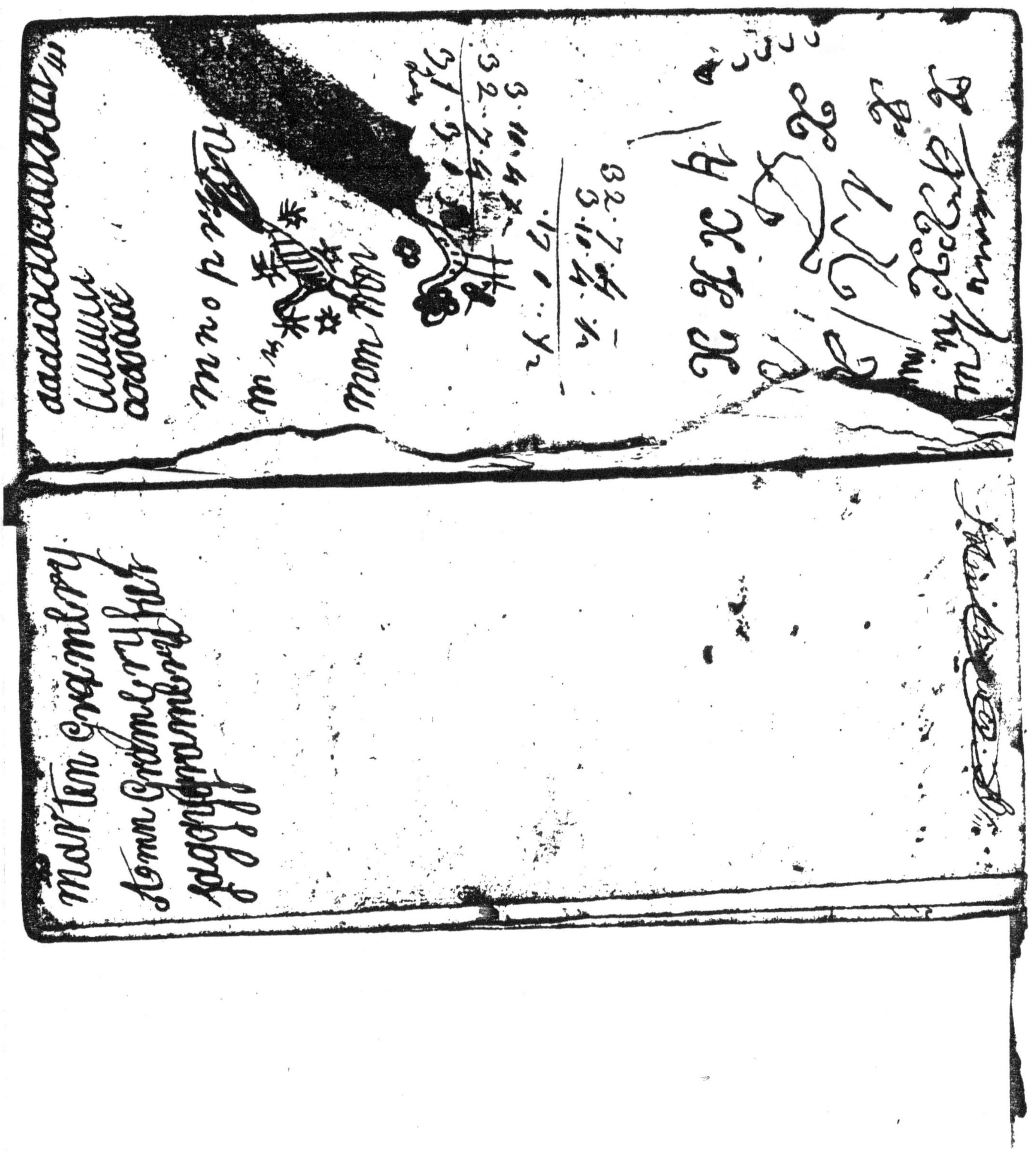

Lewis my negro boy
born December the 23 1745 AH

Charls negro boey was
born the 8 day of
October 1745 at N...

Rachel my negro gal
was born Aperdon...
the 2 day 1749

Jams ... born the
5 of June 1752

Jack anderan was
born march the 15
the too tweens 1755

Sele an tree ing
born September th...
the too tweens 175

Abigail Hargraves

Given the 26 day 43
my negro boy mustan
was born 1760

December the 15 day 1761
mary Granbery died

December 22 day 1761
little Ann ... carne
... to live

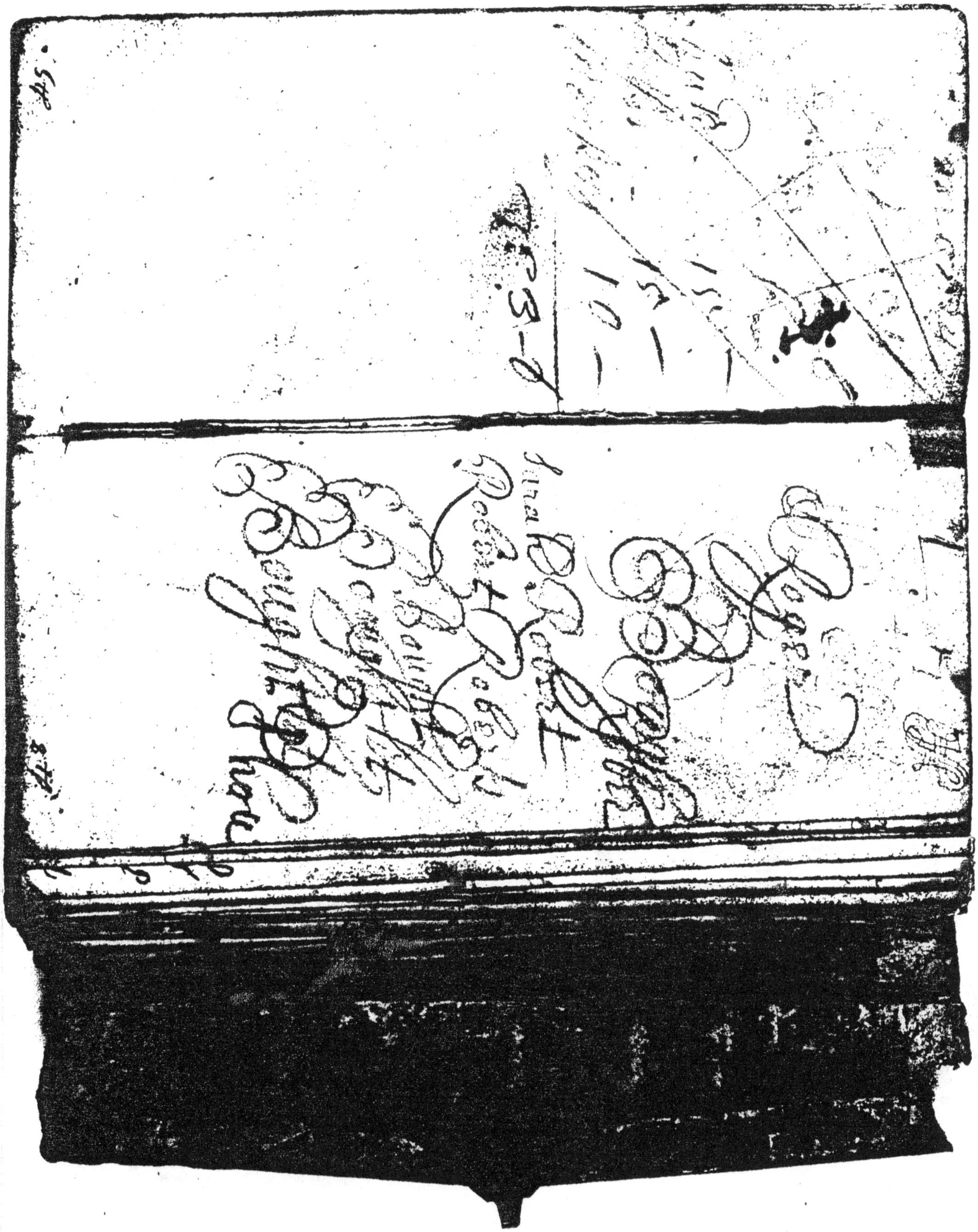

Thomas Brickel
To one pott old house
To one pistol
To one box iron

John ____ Dettor to Sarah Granbury
To 2 pound of Butter at 12
nine pound of Tobacco
2 yall of ____ ____ at 16
2 yell of floss more at 10
2 gallans of ____ ____ att 20
gallans of ____ more att 16
gallas of ____ more att
pound of ____ ____
peach of meal

Geore Langley went Away fabery 9 day
1739

William Fumner one pa...

John Knoley one pair

Adam Neeby one paire

John Karton one paire

Josiah went from here the 21 day of october to goe to Carilinca to keep stoer for Redock 1747

Jary hon cok begin to ... the 29 day of october thar fust week of the 1747

9160 1768
John Granbery 1728
book and in it
Let him Look
John Granbery
1768   20
1726

Gaill

an

...ny but

...ny and ...ny but If hen Aunny Bishon
is corn ... ...th is corn ...